SLIPPERY SNAKE

Written by

Illustrated by

Purnell

"Ah, this is the life," sighed Slippery Snake as he sunned himself on his patio one fine day. "The sun is hot, the air is sweet, and there's nobody to bother me." He had just drifted off to sleep when he heard Eager Beaver shouting from down the lane: "Yoo-hoo, Slippery Snake, I need you!"

"I might have known I wouldn't be alone for long," said Slippery Snake. "I'll pretend I'm not home."

When Eager Beaver arrived, Slippery Snake had vanished. "That's funny," he said, "I thought I saw him!"

As Eager Beaver ran off down the lane, Slippery Snake oozed towards the river bank. "Maybe I can find some peace and quiet here," he thought as he settled on the warm towel. But no sooner had he made himself comfortable than he heard shouting from across the river. "Yoo-hoo, Slippery Snake!" called Greedy Pig. "I'll be right over!"

But by the time Greedy Pig's little boat landed on the beach, Slippery Snake had gone.

"How odd," said Greedy Pig. "I know I saw Slippery Snake sunning himself here . . . didn't I?"

"It's becoming impossible to have a nice quiet day," said Slippery Snake when Greedy Pig was gone. "I might as well go into town and see a film. Nobody will look for me there. And he made himself into a perfect circle and rolled off to town. Lucky Dog saw him roll past, and thought to himself, "There goes an old bicycle tyre."

But then Slippery Snake saw Eager
Beaver coming towards him. And
Greedy Pig was coming the other way!

But by the time Eager Beaver and Greedy Pig met in front of the barber shop, Slippery Snake had gone again!

"I just don't understand it," said Eager Beaver. "I was sure Slippery Snake was at home, but then he wasn't, after all!"

"And I was sure he was on the beach," said Greedy Pig, "but then he wasn't on the beach!"

"Why exactly are you looking for me?" said a voice from on top of the barber pole.

"What's this, a talking pole?" gasped Eager Beaver.

"No, silly, it's me," said Slippery Snake, dropping down to the pavement. "Why are you both looking for me?"

"We need someone to play hide-and-seek with us," explained Greedy Pig. "Oh," said Slippery Snake. "Well, I'm not much good at that." "Then we'll hide," said Eager Beaver. "Yes, we'll hide," echoed Greedy Pig.

But they were only talking to each other – Slippery Snake had gone!